Easy Kitchen

An Adult Coloring Book

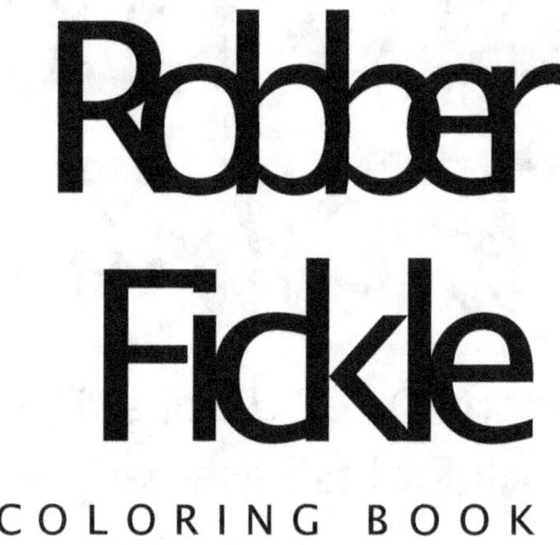

For Any Question and Suggestions
robberfickle@gmail.com

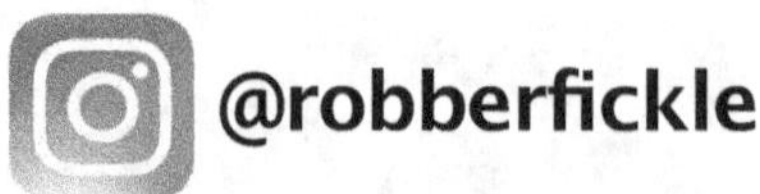

This Book Belongs To

....

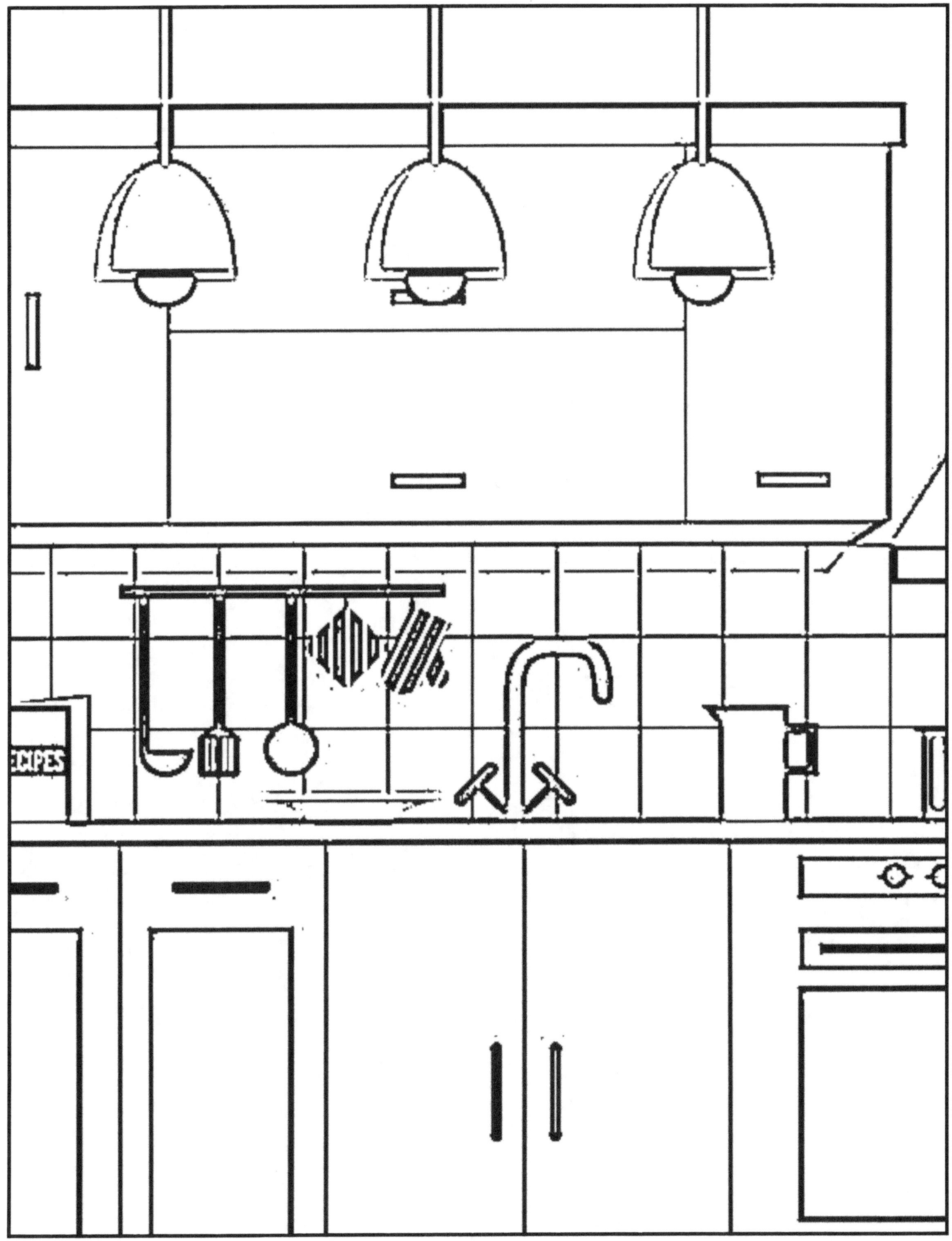

ECIPES

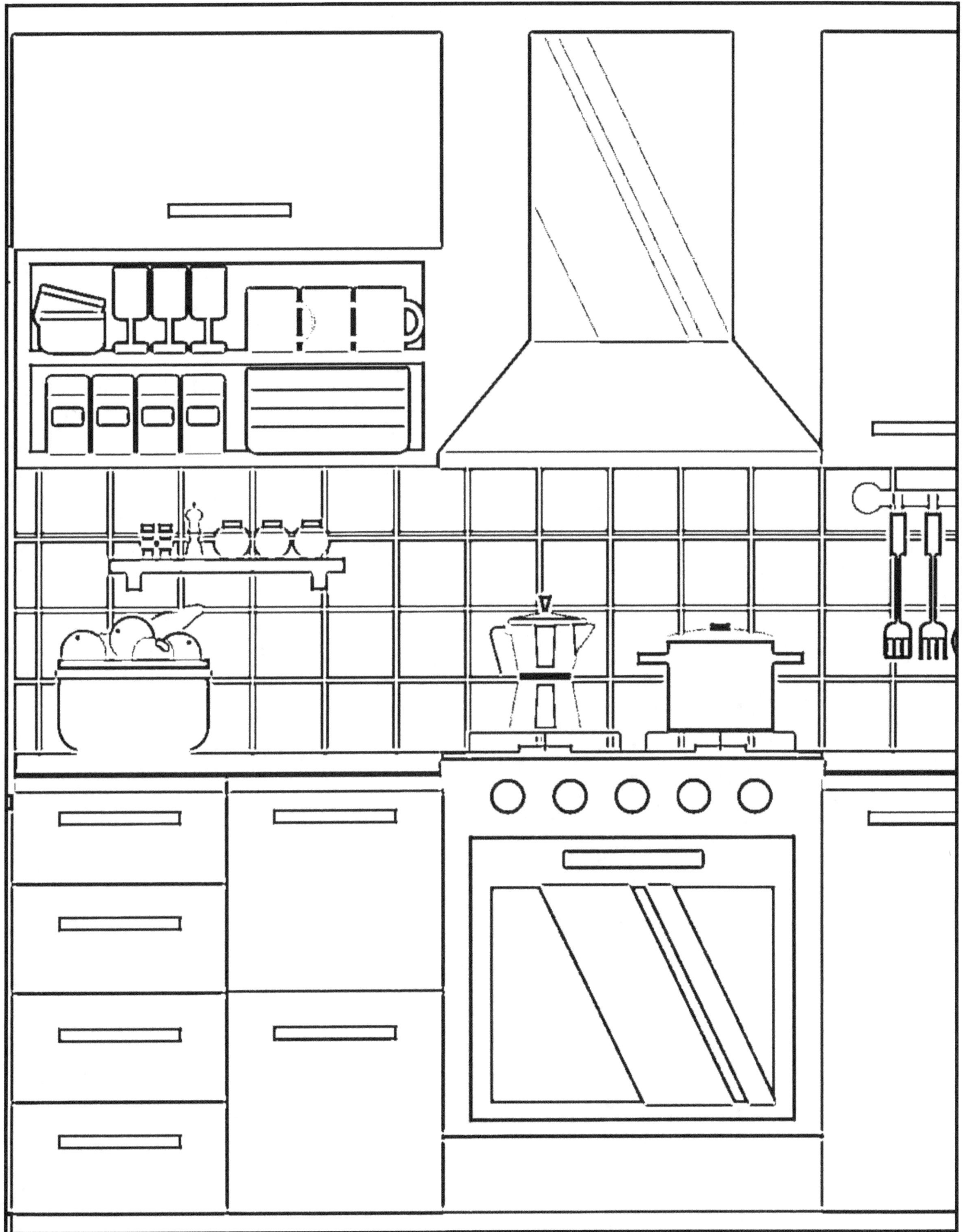

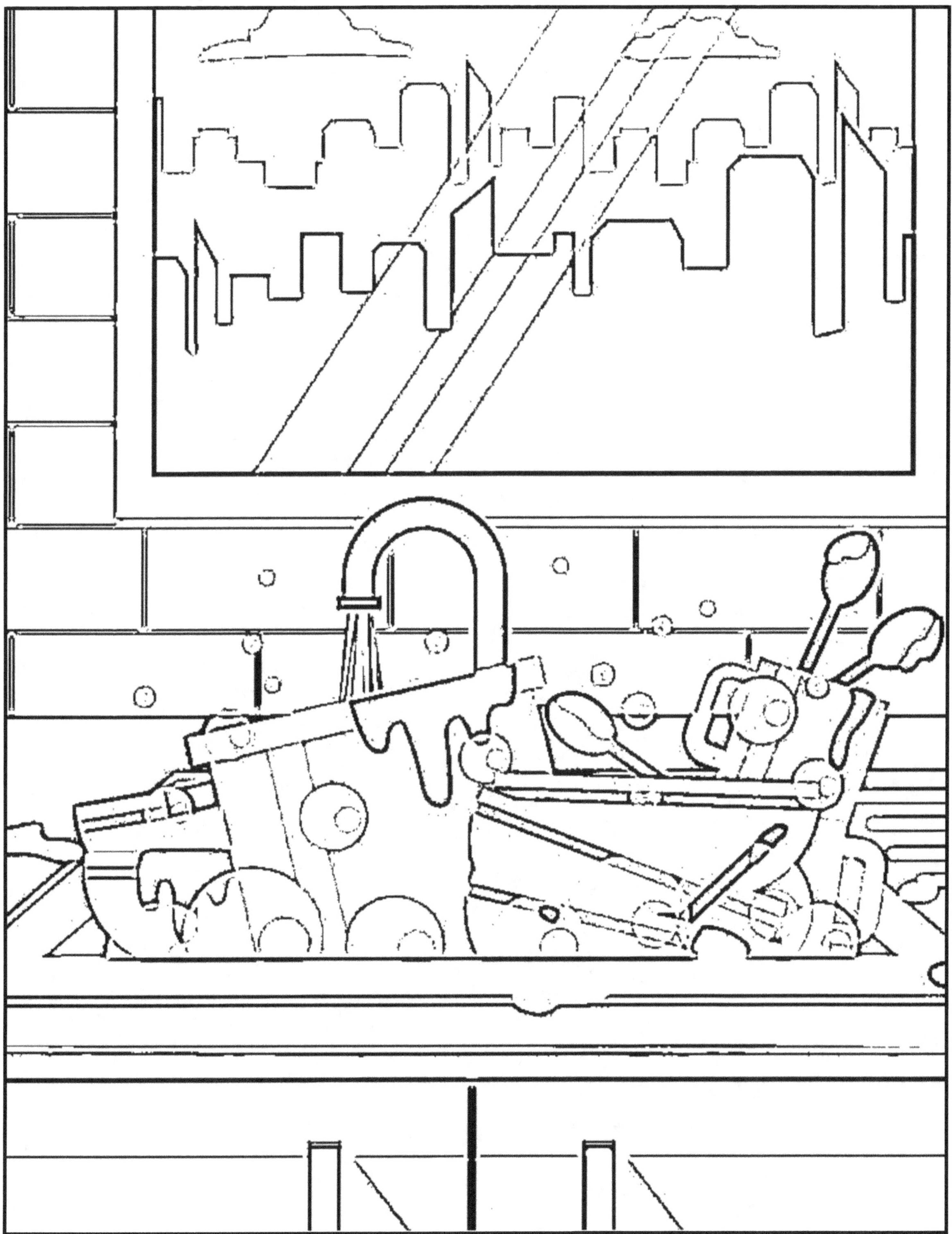

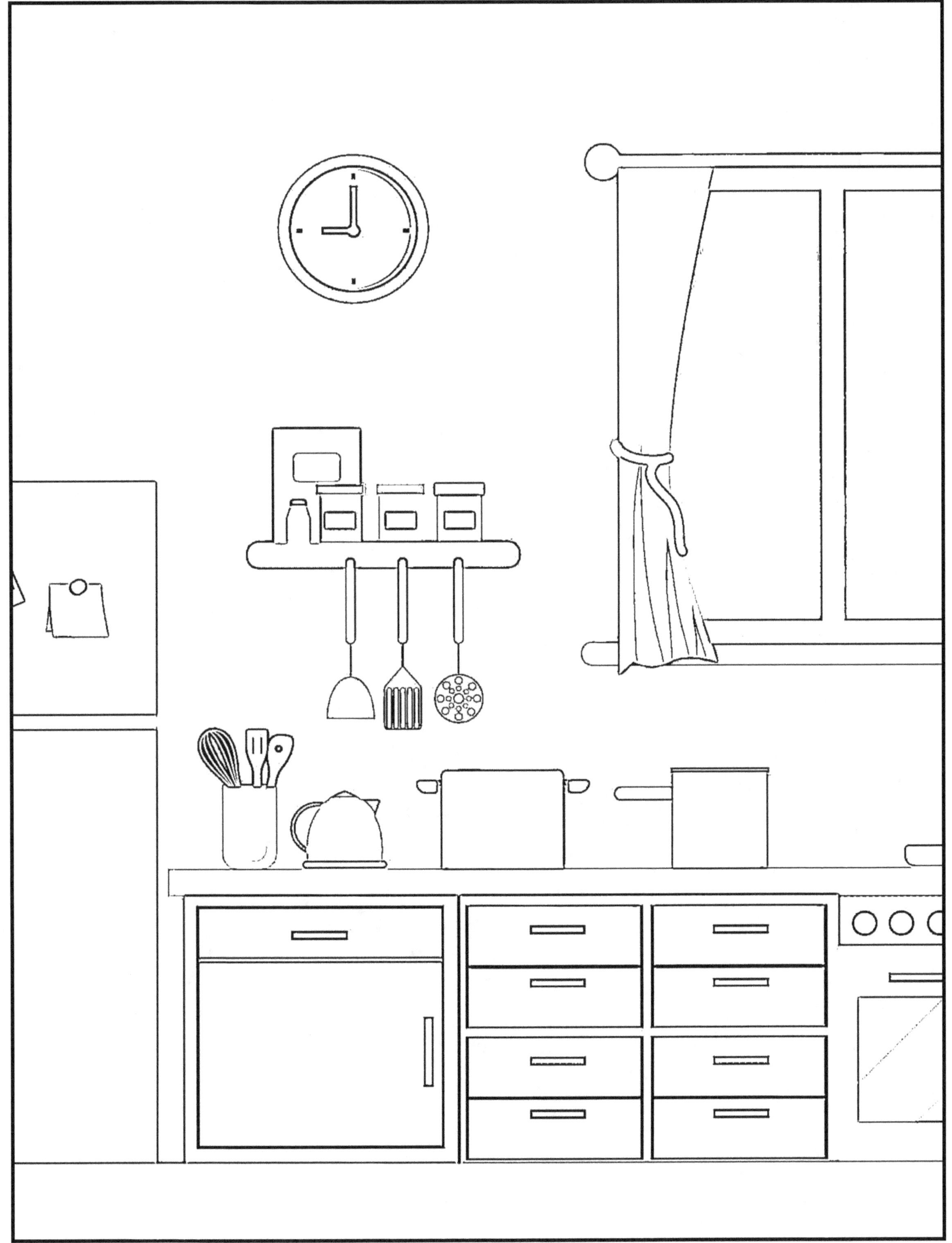

as bigger fish to fry